Seek Good, not Evil

Seek Good, not Evil
(that you may live)

SERMONS FOR THE LAST THIRD OF THE PENTECOST SEASON
(SUNDAYS IN ORDINARY TIME)

PAUL W. F. HARMS

SERIES C FIRST LESSON TEXTS FROM
THE COMMON (CONSENSUS) LECTIONARY

C.S.S. Publishing Company, Inc.
Lima, Ohio

SEEK GOOD, NOT EVIL (THAT YOU MAY LIVE)

Copyright © 1985 by
The C.S.S. Publishing Company, Inc.
Lima, Ohio

All rights reserved. No part of this publication may be reproduced, stored in a retrieval system, or transmitted in any form or by any means, electronic, mechanical, photocopying, recording, or otherwise, without the prior permission of the publisher. Inquiries should be addressed to: The C.S.S. Publishing Company, Inc., 628 South Main Street, Lima, Ohio 45804.

5860 / ISBN 0-89536-754-8   PRINTED IN U.S.A.

DEDICATION

*To the memory of Eva and John Harms —
my parents, Christians, India missionaries,
passionate educators, lovers of the Church,
lovers of Christ and loved by Christ.*

Table of Contents

A Note Concerning Lectionaries and Calendars   9

Foreword   11

Proper 22[1] Pentecost 20[2] Ordinary Time 27[3]	*Amos 5:6-7, 10-15*	*Seek Good, Not Evil (That You May Live)*	14
Proper 23 Pentecost 21 Ordinary Time 28	*Micah 1:2; 2:1-10*	*Being Wealthy, Religious and Powerful*	20
Proper 24 Pentecost 22 Ordinary Time 29	*Habakkuk 1:1-3; Habakkuk 2:1-4*	*Time and Timing*	26
Proper 25 Pentecost 23 Ordinary Time 30	*Zephaniah 3:1-9*	*The Violence Within, the Violence Without*	32
Proper 26 Pentecost 24 Ordinary Time 31	*Haggai 2:1-9*	*A Word About the Right Time*	36
Proper 27 Pentecost 25 Ordinary Time 32	*Zechariah 7:1-10*	*Religion — One Way to Get in God's Way*	42
Proper 28 Pentecost 26 Ordinary Time 33	*Malachi 4:1-6*	*There's Gotta Be a Day*	48
Christ the King	*2 Samuel 5:1-5*	*Whoever Would Be King*	54

Reformation Sunday	*Jeremiah 31:31-34*	*The Time Is Coming*	60
All Saints' Sunday	*Daniel 7:1-3, 15-18*	*Beasts, Saints and Chaos*	68
Thanksgiving Eve/ Thanksgiving Day	*Deuteronomy 26:1-11*	*To Thank Is To . . .*	76

¹*Common Lectionary*
²*Lutheran Lectionary*
³*Roman Catholic Lectionary*

A Note Concerning Lectionaries and Calendars

The following index will aid the user of this book in matching the right Sunday with the appropriate text during the second half of the church year. Days listed here include only those appropriate to the contents of this book:

Fixed-date Lectionaries

Common	Roman Catholic	Lutheran Lectionary
Proper 22 (October 2-8)	Ordinary Time 27	Pentecost 20
Proper 23 (October 9-15)	Ordinary Time 28	Pentecost 21
Proper 24 (October 16-22)	Ordinary Time 29	Pentecost 22
Proper 25 (October 23-29)	Ordinary Time 30	Pentecost 23
Proper 26 (October 30 — November 5)	Ordinary Time 31	Pentecost 24
Proper 27 (November 6-12)	Ordinary Time 32	Pentecost 25
Proper 28 (November 13-19)	Ordinary Time 33	Pentecost 26
Christ the King (Last Sunday of the church year)	Christ the King	Christ the King
		Reformation Sunday (Last Sunday in October)
All Saints' Sunday (First Sunday in November)		All Saints' Sunday (First Sunday in November)
Thanksgiving Day	Thanksgiving Day	Thanksgiving Day

FOREWORD

There is a chilling monotony about the texts in this volume (I hope that the sermons chill rather than dull). At least, parts of the texts are chilling — the parts that have to do with us. The bulk of them are directed to religious folk like us. One cannot read these texts and still say, "The problem is 'out there.' " Quite clearly, the problem is "in here." Denunciation and judgment from God and his prophets — one cannot always tell where the one ends and the other begins — needed then are as needed now. The texts teach us that we haven't learned much over the centuries nor the millenia, for that matter. In the words of Paul Scherer, "We often do not know what we ought to do because we have already decided not to do what we know we ought." It is not a matter of knowing but of doing.

The causes of the monotony are chilling, though each prophet nuances his denunciation differently. Though the prophesies may be monotonous, we ignore their monotony at our peril. We need reminding, and the prophets do remind.

There is also a cheering monotony. (I hope these sermons cheer as well as chill.) God refuses to give up on us, ever. The people of the Old Testament and we have given God all the excuses he needs, but he refuses to give up. If it ever appears so, as indeed it sometimes does, it is only for a moment that we may taste his goodness even more. The prophets match the intensity of denunciation with an equal intensity of God's compassion.

These texts are intolerant of religion that severs the indissoluble link between worship of God and serving the neighbor. They insist there is no such thing as "religion being a private affair" or "religion being what one does with one's solitude." The prophets obliterate the sonorities of these assertions. Worship is compassion/action or it is nothing.

"How are the widows, the orphans, the strangers, the oppressed, the poor, the defenseless faring?" is their refrain and their criteria. Christ mirrors the prophets' language, "Whoever offends one of these little ones offends me."

Today prophets may find their voices no more heeded than yesterday but no less needed. Hence, the ancient voices for modern eardrums with the same ancient problems need no apology.

In a way, this volume is a contradiction. A sermon is oral. This is print. One may make a movie or a videotape of a sermon. Yet neither of these really reproduces a sermon. If they cannot do so, certainly print cannot.

Print cannot capture the orchestrations of the voice, its intensity, the timing, the pace, the silences, the intonations, the emotional coloring: the responding and responsive presence of the preacher enfleshed; nor the variegated changes in the face and the eyes; the subtle or emphatic change in the posture, the intensity of concentration wherein all energies coalesce, the eye-to-eye contact with the hearer, the felt sense of communication between preacher and hearer; in short, the sight of a preacher "giving birth to Christ in the hearer."

In addition, print does not capture the presence of the hearers who are responding with gestures of their own; nor the mood of the time, the day, the very moment of preaching; nor the architecture, nor . . . nor . . . All those definitive elements that comprise that more than ninety percent as embryonic blueprint becomes sermon in that oral moment.

In print we have about ten percent of the sermon, a very important ten percent, but ten percent. In print the sermon is read, not heard. It is read silently in solitary fashion, not commonly with others. So the printed/read sermon is really a genre distinct from the preached/heard sermon, related to it, but different from it. Obviously, it can be very useful. I thought it important and helpful to call this difference to mind.

Whether these sermons are read or preached or both, they should be preceded by the reading of the text. The sermon presupposes that the tonal coloring, the reverberation of the mood and even of the sound of the text is present as the sermon moves.

Who can recognize fully all those who have contributed to one's learning about preaching the Gospel? Even after years it is still more a matter of learning than of mastery. My parents, of course, missionaries both, one ordained for the ministry, both ordained by baptism; my wife and family; Richard R. Caemmerer, Sr., my principal homiletics professor whose death I still mourn, whose inspiration will not cease: C. S. Lewis, who mastered the fusion of manner and matter in preaching the Gospel as have few others; Joseph Sittler, whose care for the preaching enterprise will not flag; and those students who have joined the venture and the adventure of preaching the Gospel, caught its joy and its divine necessity, and embrace its agony because they were enflamed by your vision, flawed as that may be.

A special word of thanks to Jill Prigan, who made her way through my serpentine hieroglyphics, the mechanically depressed voiceprint of my laryngeal offerings as revealed by audio tape, and then typed and retyped the manuscript. What there is here of virtue is hers, the flaws I claim as my own.

If this volume stretches some mind, enlarges some vision, illuminates some passion, refreshes some heart with the Gospel of the crucified and risen Christ, I would be much pleased.

Paul W. F. Harms

Seek the Lord and live, lest he break out like fire in the house of Joseph, and it devour, with none to quench it for Bethel, O you who turn justice to wormwood, and cast down righteousness to the earth! They hate him who reproves in the gate, and they abhor him who speaks the truth. Therefore because you trample upon the poor and take from him exactions of wheat, you have built houses of hewn stone, but you shall not dwell in them; you have planted pleasant vineyards, but you shall not drink their wine. For I know how many are your transgressions, and how great are your sins — you who afflict the righteous, who take a bribe, and turn aside the needy in the gate. Therefore he who is prudent will keep silent in such a time; for it is an evil time. Seek good, and not evil, that you may live; and so the Lord, the God of hosts, will be with you, as you have said. Hate evil, and love good, and establish justice in the gate; it may be that the Lord, the God of hosts, will be gracious to the remnant of Joseph.

(Amos 5:6-7, 10-15)

Amos 5:6-7, 10-15 *Proper 22 (C)*
Pentecost 20 (L)
Ordinary Time 27 (RC)

Seek Good, Not Evil (That You May Live)

Adolph Hitler had a dream of a thousand-year empire. The years may make us forget too soon and too easily the terror that was Adolph Hitler. The terror was that this little man, not in stature alone, but in smallness of mind, had managed to do in an extraordinary degree what others had done before him, and what we are all capable of doing. What he did, says Kenneth Burke, was to make virtue vice, and vice virtue. When, therefore, the Nazis put six million Jews and millions of others into the ovens, they did not do it because Adolph Hitler or anyone else was holding a gun in their backs, a matter of killing or being killed. They did not do it because the killing of millions was a moral duty. They did it, says Kenneth Burke, as an act of adoration.

As life had been treasured, under the Nazis killing was treasured. Having denied infinity to God, they became infinitized men and sought to destroy all of life or to create life somehow by an orgiastic celebration of death.

Evil had not just become an incidental and accidental accompaniment of life. Evil had become national and international policy. Death resulted not from bureaucratic bungling, but from thorough planning. So twisted had become the Nazi mind that devotion to the destruction of the Jews diverted badly needed supplies from the military and helped cripple the Nazi effort on the Russian front.

The memories of the Holocaust stand as a graphic reminder how evil can be taken for the highest good and the highest good taken for evil. It happened in our lifetime.

Is the Nazi-twisted experience instructive of the twistings of the people of this text?

They wanted life. Their method? Turning sweet justice into nausea. They hated reproof of their nausea. They abhorred those who told the truth. They trampled on the poor. It was not enough for the poor to be poor. They had to be trampled on, invited being trampled on because they were poor. While the prosperous could get loans easily, the poor were made to pay every cent with usury. Someone once said, "Capitalism for the poor, socialism for the rich." Citizens on welfare must spend frugally. Industries already wealthy are entitled to, note the word, not extravagance, but to "cost overruns."

"The religion of the eighties? Success. Compassion is out," responded a national magazine. It then proceeded to detail its answer, young men and women bent on making fortunes and spending fortunes in the most profligate way.

The righteous are afflicted, not the wrongdoer. There is a readiness to take bribes. The poor man's claims, if he dare make them public, are ignored because he is powerless to press for justice.

The language is fierce, scathing. But no matter. What should provoke denial and retaliation merits only indifference, not unlike indifference in the West. How many times has it not been said, and not by Christians alone, that the wealth of our country has come not only at the expense of other countries but at the expense of poor countries whom we have made poorer still. Is that perhaps trampling on the poor? Does it not strike us as strange that we have industries producing products which are guaranteed to have little or no food value and drinks which are guaranteed to give us no more than one calorie for every eight ounces consumed? Companies are in competition to produce more and more which gives us less and less nutrition but more pleasure, more color, more pleasing texture, more pleasing taste than ever before. Alongside that are not the hungry alone, but the starving — the Ethiopians, the Sudanese, the desperate millions of others less publicized but no less starving.

"Out of sight, out of mind," used to cover much ignorance. That is no longer possible. Television, which is blamed for much chaff and rightly so, will not let us forget the hungry, the starving, the poor, the oppressed, the disenfranchised. Television has helped us see, if not realize, our intricate interrelationship. Television will not let us escape each other, try as we may.

The struggle to remain alive is a fierce drive in all of us. Elie Wiesel, the noted chronicler of the Holocaust, records vividly a concentration camp incident — a son's beating and clawing his own father to death for a crust of bread, only then to die himself at the hands of the Nazis a few moments later. It is frightening what we will do just to maintain life a few moments longer.

To live at the expense of the other, is that life? The torrential condemnation of Amos says, "No!" The good life is not life that comes at the expense of the poor, the unfortunate, the oppressed, and the dispossessed, the lonely and the exiled.

What has contributed in part to the kind of public debauch at the expense of the poor in Amos' day and in ours is that relation to God is often felt to be a private affair. Private good behavior for all of its excellence, however, does not well reckon with structures and systems which by their very nature oppress, put the poor at a disadvantage, operate with technical and legal rights while violating the moral. It has been too easy for us to do band-aid work with a good conscience while structures and systems have continued to victimize.

We have talked about the violence *in* schools, for example, but what about the violence *of* the schools? There is violence within companies, but what about the violence *of* companies? In recent days more than one company that has served a community for decades closed its operations overnight and moved to another place where the goods can be made even more cheaply at the cost of the new workers and at the cost of the old workers left behind.

So, Amos' words are not encouraging the dressing up of a private morality. Stalin's daughter said that Stalin loved her very much. At the same time he authorized the deaths of millions of his fellow Soviet citizens.

Seek peace! Establish justice! Speak the truth! Reprove truth! Seek good, not evil that you may live!

The speaking for good is to be a passion. We are to be burned up with the desire and will that good will reign. We are to be consumed by the same kind of passion that consumed our Lord.

The purpose of the text and of this sermon is not the development of a new program in niceness. It is a seeking after life itself, as God describes and designs that life. To live, to be alive means to seek good, not evil, to establish justice, to uphold righteousness, rather than cast it down; to be exacting in charity rather than in covetousness. That's but a partial description of what it means to be alive. That is certainly what it meant to be alive for the people of Amos' time. The textual phrase is, "And the Lord God of hosts will be with you." That there is to be no mistaking about what God meant by *life,* there is the Christ. He said that life is not possible unless we lose it. And he lost his life in the pursuit of justice. His way of righting wrong was to die for us the wrongdoers that we might be justified in the eyes of God through his death. Christ did just the opposite of the people of the text. He did not make justice bitter but made it richly sweet. What a way God chose to make clear his sense of justice — to give us that which is too good to be true, to give us that which we do not deserve.

He has given us the gift of life, that is the gift of himself. That is life to give oneself for the other as he has given himself for us. Or in the words of Amos, to seek the good of others as he has sought our good, to speak the truth to others as he has spoken the truth to us, to see that the poor get their due as he has seen that we have gotten our due, to establish justice as he has dealt justly with us, to praise the righteous, to see that the needy's needs are met.

Seek good, not evil, that you may live. In short, be like God.

Hear, you peoples, all of you; hearken, O earth, and all that is in it; and let the Lord God be a witness against you, the Lord from his holy temple.

Woe to those who devise wickedness and work evil upon their beds! When the morning dawns, they perform it, because it is in the power of their hand. They covet fields, and seize them; and houses, and take them away; they oppress a man and his house, a man and his inheritance. Therefore thus says the Lord: Behold, against this family I am devising evil, from which you cannot remove your necks; and you shall not walk haughtily, for it will be an evil time. In that day they shall take up a taunt song against you, and wail with bitter lamentation, and say, "We are utterly ruined; he changes the portion of my people; how he removes it from me! Among our captors he divides our fields." Therefore you will have none to cast the line by lot in the assembly of the Lord. "Do not preach" — thus they preach — "one should not preach of such things; disgrace will not overtake us." Should this be said, O house of Jacob? Is the Spirit of the Lord impatient? Are these his doings? Do not my words do good to him who walks uprightly? But you rise against my people as an enemy; you strip the robe from the peaceful, from those who pass by trustingly with no thought of war. The women of my people you drive out from their pleasant houses; from their young children you take away my glory for ever. Arise and go, for this is no place to rest; because of uncleanness that destroys with a grievous destruction.

(Micah 1:2, 2:1-10)

Micah 1:2, 2:1-10

Proper 23 (C)
Pentecost 21 (L)
Ordinary Time 28 (RC)

Being Wealthy, Religious and Powerful

That's like the blast from the furnace of Nebuchadnezzar, who had the furnaces heated to seven times their usual intensity in order to consume Shadrach, Meshach and Abednego. It's the outpouring of a man or woman with a short fuse, a fuse which has been short for a long time.

One wonders whether or not it would have been wise to have a committee check this language before it was uttered in public, especially for a church public. That lacerating language may have its place in other places, but the church is hardly the place.

But there's more here than an irritated prophet exercising his vocal chords. We have grown too accustomed to the always cool, laid back voice of our news broadcasters, who maintain their icy calm even in the midst of catastrophic events. It makes us wonder if the catastrophic moments have occurred or not. The calm voice and the calm figure are in the foreground, the devastated Mount St. Helens in the background. The foreground takes precedence over the background.

Not so here. All the fury of the text is preceded by the significant words, "The word of the Lord." In our language, Micah is reporting what God is seeing, what God is feeling. It is not just a point of view. In fact, a great deal of the trouble is that that is precisely the way Micah's words are being heard, only as a point of view. Interesting, perhaps, but for all of that, parochial. But it's not parochial. It's God. It's not Micah. It's God.

But both God and Micah have a problem. How do you get rich folks to listen, to listen to anything but what they want to listen to? Worse than that, how do you get rich *religious* folks to listen? Let us not forget that rich defines most of us.

That's correct. After we've recovered from the first blast of fury, we realize that it is not pagan people whom God has addressed. He does so on other occasions. Here he is addressing his own people. His people who claimed the temple of Solomon as their place of worship and continued to worship and think of themselves as the people of God but had become specialists in anti-God activity of every sort. That activity included devising wickedness; brewing up new ways to do evil even when they should have been sleeping; defrauding people simply because they had the power to do so ("My first in your face" was their motto) and not only coveting a field but seizing the field they had coveted, and doing the same with houses of others, by rising up against the people of God as though the people of God were the enemy; stripping away the robes of those who would be peaceful, so that a soldier at the front was in less danger than when he fell into their hands. The totality of the outrage is complete when the most defenseless are attached by the powerful.

Has it changed much in our time? The women and the children, the special ones with whom God is concerned because he knows if their condition is favorable, the condition of all people is favorable. If their condition is not favorable, the condition of others may be ever-so-favorable, but in his eyes it is not favorable. The women and children are outraged by being driven out of their homes (such as they are), and driven into exile. Even their poor excuses for homes are seized by those who already have much more than they can possibly use even in the most profligate of their actions.

The outrage is complete. There is no evil they have imagined. There is no evil they have not imagined that they have not done. Having performed so outrageously, they cannot possibly imagine the breadth of their outrage nor can they imagine that their outrage can ever come to an end. As far as they are able to see, their outrageous behavior has brought them more and more wealth.

Both they and we have often taken prosperity as a sure sign of our Lord's benediction, its absence a sure sign of his absence. Is this perhaps why we secretly hate to be poor and fear being poor? Does it mean that God no longer cares for us?

Why, then, is it so hard to hear the disembowling words of Micah and of God? On a first level, how is it possible for one to be rich and wrong at the same time? On the face of it, it seems impossible. Wealth, affluence is a result of hard work, a just reward for careful investments, not to say coveteousness, and the rich do not use the word covet.

There are very few of us who do not want to get wealthy. Being wealthy seems a laudable goal. Just because some make it and some don't doesn't alter the equation. One of the driving forces of Western civilization, especially in the United States, is that of upward mobility. That includes wealth, as much as you can get. The rags-to-riches image is more than an image. It's a compelling force. The poor boy who makes it to the White House is one of our favorite stories. To be master and dominate others is a personal as well as a national and religious goal. Why is it that number one means so much and that number two means so little, even though in a specific area the number two person has only one more who is better than he or she is?

We forget that this inordinate pursuit of wealth comes at high cost. That fact is not much in our conversation. It is in God's however. It is in the text. It's the small folks, the little folks, the peaceful folks, the women and the children who pay the price for our greed. Human rights are subordinated to greed. The little ones of Christ's judgment day story pay the price — a price that God says is too high. Hence, Micah's message. It is not without significance that until comparatively modern times the church opposed usury, that is, loaning things on interest, that which has become the very backbone of our economic systems, borrowing other people's money with interest. How many of us would be here this morning if we had never borrowed other people's money or are not here on borrowed money?

The heights that come with money and power seem to produce deafness and historical amnesia. People in power have a way of believing that they will always be in that position. Stories of people falling from the heights are just that, stories of other people. Never mind that Muhammed Ali is no longer the greatest, that the Shah of Iran is no longer the Shah of Iran, that Howard Hughes died a miserable recluse, that Richard Nixon, once the most powerful man in the world, had to resign amidst personal and national disgrace.

Even the rapacious Romans of old had a slave constantly whisper into the ear of a conquering general in those moments of the triumphal procession down the streets of Rome, *"Sic transit gloria mundi."* Thus passes away the glory of this world.

Those of you in this congregation who are over sixty years of age have seen the disappearance of an empire that seemed untouchable. The British Empire is no more. During our lifetime it has ceased to be. Contemplate that for a moment. Teach us to number our days and apply our hearts unto wisdom. The Hitlerian empire with its dream is no more.

Carl Sandburg captured that moment in a poem in which a chorus sings, "We are the greatest nation. We are the greatest people that ever was." At the close of the poem not even the rat prints are left to tell us that this was the greatest nation, the greatest people that ever was.

But for all the good that it seems to do, Micah says, they may just as well have a drunken preacher, something they would probably resent because of their civility and sophistication, but who would represent them best of all because of their being drunk with power and greed and covetousness.

Job is an exception to much of this. It was on the good days that Job would make it a special point to sacrifice to God the best bullocks, for he understood the potential danger of the "seeming good days." We may turn to God on bad days. Job knew that good days are times of danger.

We now stand beyond the days of Micah. What he said came true. What they had done to others was done to them. "We are utterly ruined. Among our captors he divides our fields." Uncleanness has destroyed with a bitter destruction.

We have moved beyond Micah, but not beyond the conditions he describes, not beyond the message he proclaims. When the poor and the widows and the orphans end up with the short end of the stick, there can be nothing so good as to excuse that.

The message still continues among the righteous and the unrighteous. Finally God sent the Prophet of prophets, the Teacher of teachers, the Preacher of preachers — himself in the person of his Son. You know what they did to him. They cast him out of the city in hopes that they would never have to hear that message or that Messenger again. But neither crucifixion nor death could hold him. He only reconfirmed what had been said again and again. As you have done it or not done it to the least of these, you have done it or not done it to me. The alliance is not between wealth and wealth, covetousness and covetousness, but between himself and his people. The short run never seems that way. That's why covetousness gets its way. But God specializes in the long run. He believes people are more important than dollars.

He died about that, so that we might live about that: being rich toward God.

The oracle of God which Habakkuk the prophet saw. O Lord, how long shall I cry for help, and thou wilt not hear? Or cry to thee "Violence!" and thou wilt not save? Why dost thou make me see wrongs and look upon trouble? Destruction and violence are before me; strife and contention arise.

I will take my stand to watch, and station myself on the tower, and look forth to see what he will say to me, and what I will answer concerning my complaint. And the Lord answered me: "Write the vision; make it plain upon tablets, so he may run who reads it. For still the vision awaits its time; it hastens to the end — it will not lie. If it seems slow, wait for it; it will surely come, it will not delay. Behold, he whose soul is not upright in him shall fail, but the righteous shall live by his faith.

(Habakkuk 1:1-3, 2:1-4)

Habakkuk 1:1-3, 2:1-4

Proper 24 (C)
Pentecost 22 (L)
Ordinary Time 29 (RC)

Time and Timing

"Why do bad things happen to good people?" is the way we say it today. "Why art thou silent when the wicked swallow up the man more righteous than he is?" It is not only "Why do bad things happen to good people?" but why does a holy and a righteous God permit the unrighteous to swallow the righteous, the wicked to devour the innocent? It may happen, but why does God permit it, seemingly doing nothing about it?

It is bad enough if some outsider is the villain. It is intolerable when the villain is home-grown. What response is left to us if some of our own turn on us and do so deliberately, premeditatedly, simply because they are in a position to do so? It's like having the firemen start the fires, the policemen rob the banks and murder the citizenry, the government extort money from its subjects, and the armed forces ravage their own country. Outsiders we could excuse by saying they are outsiders, but how does one excuse the insiders?

For all we did to the South Vietnamese, the Cambodians and the Laotians, certainly Vietnamese must ask why they are imprisoned in Vietnam prisons, the Laotians in Laotian prisons, the Cambodians in Cambodian prisons — political prisoners imprisoned for what they are thinking.

Why, not so incidentally, do we find the chiefs of state so often professing a love of their country and a dislike, not to say hostility, for their countrymen? The ultimate poignancy is Christ's outcry from the cross, "My God, my God, why hast Thou forsaken *me!*" As difficult, as unsatisfactory as are any of the answers, the question is legitimized if our Lord himself in the moment of extremity after dedicated life to his Father should ask the same question, "My God, my God, why hast thou forsaken me!" Why should God turn on the one who without question has been faithful? The fact that he does, makes it a question of supreme importance. Easy explanations are out.

How does one excuse God, the righteous God, for letting the righteous be victimized at will by those who scorn him and them? That's the problem that angers and humiliates Habakkuk. Outraged by what God's people are doing to God's people, he is even more outraged that God is doing nothing about it.

Who of us can understand God's ways the way we would like? For one thing, God has not chosen to tell us the whole story of himself. He's given us the central story but not the whole story. Whatever he has not spoken we speak for him, then demand *he* act the way *we* do. We have a black/white, on/off, binary idea of the way God should right wrongs, especially if someone has wronged us. Instant action! Instant justice! Instant retaliation!

Do we ask for the same quick, immediate solution when we are the ones who have wronged, when we have been unjust, when we have used power to serve self? It's a different matter then, isn't it? Then we are quick to plead extenuating circumstances, give explanations, beg for forgiveness. Then we are not unlike the criminal who refuses to extend mercy to his victim but who pleads weepingly for mercy when he himself is caught. Perhaps God might be rejecting the instantaneous response because that would mean sweeping all aside, not just the so-called guilty. That's what the story of the flood is all about. Sweep away the "baddies." Keep the "goodies." Then God discovers that the few whom he had saved were not as good as he thought.

Instantaneous rightings of wrongs has its drawbacks, mostly for those who demand that kind of action.

Perhaps we also get trapped in the old illusions that some obvious, public wrongs are worse than those that remain private. Hence, it is easy to demand justice be done to those whose wrongs are public and grievous while private offenders appear innocent.

God also understands time differently than we do. Since we measure in milliseconds, a little time seems like a lot of time. In our demand for justice *now* we forget that God is the inventor, the creator of time; so his relationship to time differs from that of our own. "A thousand years are as one day, and one day as a thousand years."

So, the people of Israel can be in bondage in Egypt for an inordinate number of years. They cry out to God to free them. Then God remembers his promises to Abraham, Isaac and Jacob. When did that promising take place? Only four hundred years before. And his delivery of the people of Israel is regarded as fulfilling his promise four hundred years before that deliverance. That's a different way of keeping a promise.

A guide at the Wailing Wall in Jerusalem explained it this way: A devout Jew who lives far from Jerusalem has his heart set on getting to the Wailing Wall during his lifetime. He dies without having made the journey. Then his children take up the wish and the dream. They do not make it. Then the grandchildren. They are not successful. Then the great-grandchildren, the great-great-great-grandchildren. At last one of the great-great-great-great-grandchildren does get to the Wailing Wall. In the person and presence of this child, the hopes and the dreams of all that went before her are fulfilled. The devout father who died several hundred years before is at the Wailing Wall as much as the child who now prays there. That is why God said that he had fulfilled his promise to Abraham, to Isaac and to Jacob when we would say he only fulfilled it for those Hebrews he brought out of Egypt some four hundred years later.

Individualism has become such a strong religion in the West that we cannot work very well with the idea that promises made to us, hopes held high by us, dreams which are dreamt by us are really all fulfilled when they come true in the life of our progeny generations later, because we were never able to taste them personally.

That's not unlike God's timetable with retribution.

Do we really believe that God takes no pleasure in the death of the wicked? Note the language: it does not say, "takes no pleasure in the death of his saints," but "takes no pleasure in the death of the wicked." How does that sit with us who gloat, rejoice over the punishment, the comeuppance of such as Richard Nixon, too clever for his own good, the downfall of a John DeLorean; the suicide of an Adolph Hitler; the stroke-induced death of a Joseph Stalin; or even, on a much lesser scale, the crushing of a sports hero by one still younger, or by the process of aging; when the so-called great are, as we say, brought down to our level, the victims of alcoholism, or a dissolute life.

Oh, yes, we rejoice over the death of the wicked. The more righteous we sense ourselves to be, the more fully and freely we gloat.

But not God. He takes no pleasure in the death of the wicked. Always with God there is the hope that the wicked would turn from their way and live. That the wicked would seek good and not evil. God does not give up easily, though it may seem so to us.

"The vision has its time; it hastens to the end — it will not lie. If it seems so, wait for it; it will surely come, it will not delay." We are talking different languages here. Four hundred years is a long time for the promise to be fulfilled for Abraham, Isaac, and Jacob. Some two hundred years of slavery is a long time for the black man in America. Add to that, years of not-quite-freedom since the Emancipation Proclamation, and you've got more time. Two years is a long time in a concentration camp. One year is too long. One day is too long. Yet people have spent whole lifetimes in the gulags of Russia.

The delay between the sin of Adam and Eve and the coming of Christ is a long time. Three days on the cross is a long time, especially after you have first been beaten until the white of your backbone and the white of your ribs show through the mangled flesh that once covered them.

As if to heighten the confusion even more, what Christ seems to designate as injustice — "My God, my God, why has Thou forsaken me?" — God called the real understanding of justice, different than any other understanding of it. To give the wicked what they have coming to them is nothing else but routine. But what if the wicked and the guilty got justice by not getting what they had coming to them; namely, Christ; namely, grace; namely, a new life?

"For I am not ashamed of the Gospel," writes Paul. "It is the saving power of God for everyone who has faith, the Jew first, but the Greek also — because here is revealed God's way of righting wrong, a way that starts from faith and ends in faith: as the Scripture says, 'He who is righteous by faith shall live.' " (Romans 16:17)

And again, "But now, quite independently of law, God's justice has been brought to life. The law and the prophets both bear witness to it; it is God's way of righting wrong, effective through faith in Christ for all who have faith — all, without distinction. For all alike have sinned, and are deprived of the divine splendor, and all are justified by God's free grace alone, through his act of liberation in the person of Christ Jesus. For God designed him to be the means of expiating sin by his sacrificial death, effective through faith. God meant by this to demonstrate his justice now in the present, showing that he is both himself just and justifies anyone who puts his faith in Jesus."

The cry against injustice must not stop. God's cry in Christ is the greatest cry of all. The work of righting injustice must not stop. God is working harder than all of us. But perhaps the question at the beginning needs to be rephrased, and with that rephrasing comes a little more vision.

Will I ever fully recover from the amazement of God's patience with me? The ultimate patience he has with me in Christ? How does he do it? Why does he do it? He not only does not take any pleasure in the death of the wicked, his innocent dies so that the wicked may live.

Just think of it. We are among the wicked who live justified by faith in Christ who died for us and rose again. In the deepest sense of the question, "Why do such good things happen to such *bad* people?"

Woe to her that is rebellious and defiled, the oppressing city! She listens to no voice, she accepts no correction. She does not trust in the Lord, she does not draw near to her God. Her officials within her are roaring lions; her judges are evening wolves that leave nothing till the morning. Her prophets are wanton, faithless men, her priests profane what is sacred, they do violence to the law. The Lord within her is righteous, he does no wrong; every morning he shows forth his justice, each dawn he does not fail; but the unjust knows no shame.

"I have cut off nations; their battlements are in ruins; I have laid waste their streets so that none walks in them; their cities have been made desolate without a man, without an inhabitant. I said, 'Surely she will fear me, she will accept correction; she will not lose sight of all that I have enjoined upon her.' But all the more they were eager to make all their deeds corrupt." "Therefore wait for me," says the Lord, "for the day when I arise as a witness. For my decision is to gather nations, to assemble kingdoms, to pour out upon them my indignation, all the heat of my anger; for in the fire of my jealous wrath all the earth shall be consumed.

"Yea, at that time I will change the speech of the peoples to a pure speech, that all of them may call on the name of the Lord and serve him with one accord."

(Zephaniah 3:1-9)

Zephaniah 3:1-9

Proper 25 (C)
Pentecost 23 (L)
Ordinary Time 30 (RC)

The Violence Within, The Violence Without

I will utterly sweep away everything from the face of the earth. I will sweep away man and beast. I will sweep away the birds of the air and the fish of the sea. I will overthrow the wicked. I will cut off mankind from the face of the earth. I will stretch out my hand against Judah and against all the inhabitants of Jerusalem. I will punish the officials and the kings' sons. And I will punish those who fill their master's house with violence and fraud.

That's hardly the kind of talk our children hear in Sunday church school. What a torrent of outrage and anger! What a volcanic eruption of vitriol! The devastation is to be complete, nothing and no one is to be spared. God will pass judgment on all that he has made. God will make a sacrifice of people. For Israel, sacrifice was no dictionary word. Vivifying it was the experience of seeing the blood of bulls and goats and calves running in gutters in the temple. There was the compelling color of red, the warmth and aroma of blood newly spilled. Sacrifice of people, therefore, is even more horrendous. It is intentional.

The bluntness of the prophet makes us want to crawl out from under in any way possible. "This goes back to the time when religion was still in its cruder developing form," we say. "Even God was in the process of maturing and developing an identity." So these shocking words take on an historical interest, but hardly a personal one, hardly a contemporary one. In a moment the volcanic rage of the text is forgotten.

The ease of crawling out from under shows how deep and elusive is our problem. Life goes on. Religion continues. Worship continues. And officially, too. The form is maintained, the substance gutted. Only the prophet noticed.

In recent years, we've been shocked by some of the stories of the crudities, not to say savagery, emerging from the resurgent Muslim faith. And it's happening right now. It should make us recall the time of the Inquisition, when in the name of the Father, the Son, and the Holy Spirit, people were tortured, executed, burned at the stake.

"If ever that book which I am not going to write is written," says C. S. Lewis, "it must be the full confession by Christendom of Christendom's specific contribution to the sum of human cruelty and treachery. Large areas of 'the World' will not hear us until we have publicly disowned much of our past. Why should they? We have shouted the name of Christ and enacted the service of Moloch."

Writes Charles Williams, "Deep, deeper than we believe, lie the roots of sin. It is in the good that they exist; it is in the good that they thrive and send up sap and produce the dark fruit of hell. The peacock fans of holy and austere popes drove the ashes of burning men over Christendom. The torch that had set light to the crosses in the Vatican gardens of Nero did not now pass into helpless or hesitating hands." If we did not suffer from historical amnesia, we would remember the Thirty Years War between Catholics and Protestants, which devastated most of Europe at the time. If we did not suffer from historical amnesia, we would remember the bombing of Hiroshima and Nagasaki, the bombing of Dresden and the bestiality of Auschwitz, crimes which were committed in the high name of nationalism and racial superiority.

So little effect has all this devastation had on most governments, that there's actual talk of a "winnable limited nuclear war." That's language for something that has no basis in fact — a "winnable" limited nuclear war! The policy of killing people in order to solve problems continues its sacred, can we say with the language of the text, *idolatrous* course, virtually untouched by the whole history of the futility of that policy. In one of our later ventures some fifty-seven thousand Americans died in Vietnam and countless more Vietnamese. It was not unusual for ancestors, persecuted, having fled to this country to persecute others. The persecuted soon became the persecutors.

What have the South Africans learned from the United States' experience with slavery? The answer is: little or nothing. There the subjugation of the blacks has the benediction of some churches, just as slavery had its benedictions from many churches here.

The list could go on. It is important to see that the text is not exaggerating when it speaks of violence and fraud in the name of religion. If violence and the cruder forms of murder and temple prostitution are not our problem, then the fraud and violence may appear in more subtle and even more devastating forms. The refinement of Pharisaic violence and fraud is one form. The doctrine of "What's the use? what good will it do anyhow?" is another. The plain, ordinary "giving up" is another. The fancy words for it are anomie, acidia, indifference, malaise, boredom.

"Not Pilate, not Herod, not Caiaphas, not Judas fastened on Jesus Christ the reproach of insipidity," writes Dorothy Sayers. "That was left for pious hands to inflict. To make of His story something that could neither startle, nor shock, nor terrify is to crucify the Lord of glory afresh . . . Let me tell you, you good Christian people, a writer of nursery tales would be ashamed to treat a nursery tale the way you have treated the greatest story of all time."

"Nothing is so deadly as dealing with the outsides of holy things," says George MacDonald. Where is that "strong following of the Lord?" Where is "that strong seeking of the Lord, of inquiring of him?" Is it not the violence of indifference and privatism that brings on a crude kind of violence? The violence of "religion is only a private affair" often begets or permits the public disregard of the neighbor.

There is fraud when the Living Lord is not present.

There is fraud when compassion is not present.

There is fraud when the cross of Christ is not present.

More stringent than all the stringency of the text is that of 1 Corinthians 13: "If I had the tongues of men and of angels . . . if I had faith so that I could move mountains . . . if I bestow all my goods to feed the poor . . . if I give my body to be burned and have not charity, I am nothing." Paul was a living example of this — Pharisee of the Pharisees, Hebrew of the Hebrews, as touching the law perfect. Because his zeal did not know love, he violated the name of God Almighty in the name of God Almighty.

What shall we say to all this?

Nothing!

The first response is silence. Be silent before the Lord God. The noise of religion and solemn assemblies must cease as well as the violence of the non-religious world. So pervasive is this violence inside and outside religion that Paul Tournier calls it "our endemic disease."

It would seem that God has no other choice but to meet violence with violence, not in the manner of the text, but in a manner never dreamed of, before. It is still hard to believe, after. Can we say that God violated himself in the crucifixion? What else was that but violence of a most brutal kind? But this violence was different than the usual violence-vengeance-revenge-violence cycle. This time God would take the violence within himself, a violence not limited to megatons of TNT or Hiroshima devastations, but the violence of all time and all places for all time and for all eternity.

The magnitude of the resulting stench was such that God withdrew from God. He did to himself what we like to do to each other. In the process, he killed himself. He sought in this self-immolation to hold up before us what it is we do to ourselves and to each other, to tell us that we need be violent no more, heed it whether we will or no.

Every time someone is baptized, all the fury of the cross of Christ is released into the life of the newly baptized and by recollection of their own baptism, to the already baptized. God violated that we might violate no more. We are baptized into his death. His death means that violence and fraud need no longer be our stock in trade.

But God did not stop there. He provides a meal which is both a celebration of violence and of violence conquered, recycled so that instead of destruction, it produces life. What else do those graphic words mean? "This is my body, broken for you. This is my blood, shed for you. This is the new covenant in my blood. Do this in remembrance of me." Living in this violent age of potential nuclear winter, we cannot too often celebrate the feast of violence conquered, of violence prevention. This festival of violence recycled breaks the cycle which has bedeviled us ever since Cain.

Not even the wrath of a Zephaniah, as he speaks for God, even a God of violence, is up to the task. Only when God turns violence on himself, takes our endemic disease and treats it with the crucifixion and death of his Son, is there a breakthrough, a resurrection.

Each time we celebrate the festivals of contained, recycled and conquered violence — the festivals of baptism and the Lord's Supper — God affirms that there need be violence no more.

Be silent before the Lord God! Amen

In the second year of Darius the king, in the seventh month, on the twenty-first day of the month, the word of the Lord came by Haggai the prophet, "Speak now to Zerubbabel the son of Shealtiel, governor of Judah, and to Joshua the son of Jehozadak, the high priest, and to all the remnant of the people, and say, 'Who is left among you that saw this house in its former glory? How do you see it now? Is it not in your sight as nothing? Yet now take courage, O Zerubbabel, says the Lord; take courage, O Joshua, son of Jehozadak, the high priest; take courage all you people of the land, says the Lord; work, for I am with you, says the Lord of hosts, according to the promise that I made you when you came out of Egypt. My Spirit abides among you; fear not. For thus says the Lord of hosts: Once again, in a little while, I will shake the heavens and the earth and the sea and the dry land; and I will shake all nations, so that the treasures of all nations shall come in, and I will fill this house with splendor, says the Lord of hosts. The silver is mine, and the gold is mine, says the Lord of hosts. The latter splendor of this house shall be greater than the former, says the Lord of hosts; and in this place I will give prosperity, says the Lord of hosts.' "

(Haggai 2:1-9)

Haggai 2:1-9 *Proper 26 (C)*
Pentecost 24 (L)
Ordinary Time 31 (RC)

A Word About the Right Time

It's good to see that God gets what he wants, once in a while. The events of this text differ from those we've heard of the last Sundays. Here there is no rampant trampling on the poor, no idolatrous affluence, no thwarting of justice against which Micah, Zephaniah and Haggai railed.

A remnant of people had returned to Israel some eighteen years before from exile, an exile imposed by Darius and then relieved by Cyrus. Eighteen years is not a long time to resettle after your country has been devastated. Things were not going too well, chapter one tells us. They were sowing much and harvesting little, eating but never having enough; drinking but never being full; clothing themselves yet they were never warm; earning wages but putting them into a bag with holes. It was a situation altogether unsatisfactory for them to add the worries of temple-building, certainly on the face of it.

It's worth noting that God takes credit for their not doing well. He's had a hand in it. It wasn't as we say, "Just the luck of the draw." Why had he done so? God answers his own question: "Even when things are not going well, I will ask that first things be first, namely, that I be first. Obviously, I am not first if my house lies in ruins while you busy yourselves, each with his own house."

In other times and other places wealth, affluence, success threatened to pull the people away from God. In this case, hardship threatened to do the same thing. Have you ever wondered why the poor people of the world do not automatically flock to Christ? George MacDonald says, "If it be things that slay, what difference if it be things they have or things they have not?" In the case of the poor it is things that they have not that keep them away.

Being poor, the poor say, "First, let us establish ourselves. Then we will build a house for the Lord." Sounds like the yuppies of the eighties: look out for the self, get the proper education, be sure the salary is one thousand dollars for every year of your life, delay marriage; and once married, delay children, and then at the right moment . . . Why build a church when your own home leaves much to be desired? Delay makes sense.

We have our own version of delay. It is persuasive, reasonable, thoughtful, and religious. Our version is, "You have to love yourself well enough before you can hope to love others." What sounds persuasive, reasonable, thoughtful and religious is in fact self-centered. The Biblical way is that it is in loving others that the love one wants to store up for oneself comes to be. It is in losing one's life that one finds it. So delay doesn't make the deepest sense.

Not in this case. Delay here meant, "God is coming in second, and he cannot come in second even for those who are less than well off. He always asks first place. So now is the time." Paul Scherer had a good word about the preacher and time: "Because preaching takes time, the preacher makes time — which is the only way I know to have time."

"Now is that time," says Haggai. "Now is that time," says God.

What God was asking was not in some self-centered way to have a house for himself just as they wanted houses for themselves. It was rather in their working together in the building of the new temple that they would once more become aware of him, become aware of the meaning of community, become aware of each other and their need for each other, and their need for God and God's desire to give them the riches of his presence.

Many a congregation and, perhaps, you as a member of this congregation or of another, have had that precise experience. You with others gave priority to building a house of worship and discovered with all the work the splendid benedictions that came through it all. They were unlooked for, but there they were. And it came from working together with other Christians for a common goal. When the building was finished, wasn't there a feeling of regret as well as elation, elation because the building was completed, regret because the times of mutual coming together were no more?

The priority that God is asking of time and resources for himself is not for himself alone. Rather, in that strange mathematics or chemistry of his, he thus is enabled to give us more of himself. Above all else, that is what he wishes to do. "Work, for I am with you," says the Lord of hosts, "according to the promise I made with you when you came out of Egypt. My Spirit abides with you, fear not, take courage."

Some wanted to hold back because they were afraid the splendor of the new temple would not match that of the old. Not so, says God. "I will fill this house with splendor." That is, with himself and his gifts. His Spirit is there; that is, his life, love, joy, peace, and kindness.

The One who is filling the house with splendor is the One who brought them up out of the land of Egypt, that momentous event which would thereafter touch all other events. *That* God who brought them out with a mighty hand and a stretched out arm, it was he, none other, who would be with them. The language of gold and silver is used to persuade the doubters of the fullness of his love and presence. "All of the gold and silver from the ends of the earth are mine and I'm giving them to you. And you shall have prosperity. You shall have prosperity of a kind you have not known."

"To be with you . . ." What good news to hear in these days of loneliness and exile and alienation. The One who made and kept the Egyptian release pledge to Haggai, continues to make it to us and to keep it. Emmanuel, "God with us," not just a friend or a neighbor or a parent or a brother or a sister or even a lover, but God with us. God guarantees it in a strange way, sends our Companion on the way to the cross. It's confusing until we realize that by that action he is saying, "You can't name a time or a place where I cannot be with you. Even death cannot separate us."

Because his people were in exile under Darius and Cyrus, it did not mean He ceased to be with them, as at first they thought. He went with them into exile. He was with them in exile. He returned with them from exile. He was with them after exile.

So it is with us. We may have less than we ought, less than we would like to have. We may not love ourselves the way we ought. We would wait until we do things properly for ourselves.

In that moment God comes to us and says, "Don't you know who I am? Don't you know the One who brought you out of Egypt?

Don't you know who is the chief of exiles? My Son, crucified outside the city walls as a criminal outcast? And he is my pledge to you. There is no time, there is no place where anyone can be that I cannot be."

"And I saw the holy city, the new Jerusalem, coming down out of heaven from God, prepared as a bride adorned for her husband, and I heard a great voice from the throne saying, 'Behold the dwelling of God is with men. He will dwell with them and they shall be his people, and God himself will be with them.'

"And I saw no temple in the city, for its temple is the Lord God, the Almighty and the Lamb. And the city has no need of sun or moon to shine upon it, for the glory of God is its light, and its lamp the Lamb." (Revelation)

Remember, it all happened, it all came to be because we trusted His timing instead of ours.

In the fourth year of King Darius, the word of the Lord came to Zechariah in the fourth day of the ninth month, which is Chislev. Now the people of Bethel had sent Sharezer and Regemmelech and their men, to entreat the favor of the Lord, and to ask the priests of the house of the Lord of hosts and the prophets, "Should I mourn and fast in the fifth month, as I have done for so many years?" Then the word of the Lord of hosts came to me; "Say to all the people of the land and the priests, When you fasted and mourned in the fifth month and in the seventh, for these seventy years, was it for me that you fasted? And when you eat and when you drink, do you not eat for yourselves and drink for yourselves? When Jerusalem was inhabited and in prosperity, with her cities round about her, and the South and the lowland were inhabited, were not these the words which the Lord proclaimed by the former prophets?" And the word of the Lord came to Zechariah, saying, "Thus says the Lord of hosts, render true judgments, show kindness and mercy each to his brother, do not oppress the widow, the fatherless, the sojourner, or the poor; and let none of you devise evil against his brother in your heart."

(Zechariah 7:1-10)

Zechariah 7:1-10

Proper 27 (C)
Pentecost 25 (L)
Ordinary Time 32 (RC)

Religion — One Way to Get in God's Way

Another clash between religion and the worship of God. To put it another way, "The Bible is anti-religious because it is pro-God." That statement strikes at some of our most cherished traditions. Isn't religion automatically pro-God? Both the Old and New Testaments say, "Not automatically so." The Bible takes issue not only with the pagan religions, it takes issue with the religion of God's people when their religion puts God in second place. Christ said of some of the religious leaders who worshiped regularly in the temple, "They forclose mortgages on widow's houses. Their cover-up? Long prayers."

This twisting of worship comes about, says Evelyn Underhill, "Because God is invisible; worship must, therefore, be concrete." For example, when we worship God, we bow the head, close the eyes, bend the knee. These actions are second nature. They range from the simplest of such actions to the most ornate and complex imaginable, using buildings of surpassing grandeur, responding to music of the most ethereal kind.

It is this concrete action, inescapable as it is, that all too easily becomes the focus for its own sake. "Should they continue fasting?" was the question of the people of Zechariah's time. It was a seventy-year practice which reminded them of the destruction of the temple. "No," says Zechariah, that is not at the heart of God's desires. "Then the word of the Lord of hosts came to me; 'Say to all the people of the land and the priests, when you fasted and mourned in the fifth month and in the seventh, for these seventy years, was it for me that you fasted? And when you eat and when you drink, do you not eat for yourselves and drink for yourselves?' " You can see how the very thoughtful practice of fasting took them off course. What's the solution? Zechariah says, "Render true judgments, show kindness and mercy each to the other, do not oppress the widow, the fatherless, the sojourner, or the poor; and let none of you devise evil against his brother in your heart." That's but a variation on, "Thou shalt love the Lord thy God with all thy heart, with all thy soul, with all thy strength and with all thy mind." The second is much like the first, "Thou shalt love thy neighbor as thyself."

What does it mean to love God in that way? It means to love the neighbor. That's a hard statement. We easily respond to the first, recoil from the second. Yet the words of the text are action words. They don't call for a committee, or discussion, or the tracing of the origin and the problems of evil. They call for action: render; do; see that it is done.

To love is to treat people the way we want to be treated, the way God would treat them because both they and we are God's representatives to each other and for each other. The neighbor is not to be dealt with as we will. Not our keeping of fasts or some other religious duty, but the decisions and actions we take toward people determines what our religion is, what our worship life is.

Zechariah's message from God is one of compassion, "a keen awareness of the interdependence of all those living beings, which are all part of one another and involved in one another," according to Thomas Merton. To render true judgment is to give people an even break, to give them what they have coming. They don't owe us thanks. We are not bestowing something special on them. They are only receiving what is properly theirs, which had always been theirs. Neither the Emancipation Proclamation of Abraham Lincoln nor of the United States gave the black man a gift, as though he had no claim on freedom or liberty. He was but receiving that which was already his and had always been his but which had wrongfully been taken away from him. To show kindness is to serve the neighbor in such a way that it is beneficial for him.

Such is the breadth of our action and doing that it is utterly inclusive and non-restrictive, not only the brother or the sister with whom we have a close family relationship, but the widow, the fatherless, the alien, the poor. Gone from Zechariah's thinking are any such thoughts as, "As soon as I am doing well, then . . ., as long as my family is doing well, then . . . , or once the unemployment rate drops to 10%, we need not bother, or the trickle-down economic theory works. If we take care of the rich, we hope the poor will get theirs later."

No matter how good things look statistically by business, industry, or government measures, they are not good enough in God's eyes until *all* are faring well. How are the defenseless? The fatherless? The poor? The alien? The widow? Walter Brueggemann states that the Old Testament sees chaos present despite the appearance of peace as long as the widows and orphans are not getting a square shake. God makes that claim and that accusation because we are one family.

For God and, consequently, for us, there are no states and nationalities, no countries or boundaries which separate us from each other. Most have denied that most of the time. Sometimes the church itself has been no less guilty in denying we are all brothers and sisters.

If we are brothers and sisters, a sense of fairness is the only way we may deal with one another on a one-to-one basis. A sense of fairness would do much, especially in those casual meetings which seem to be of no consequence.

But we are slowly becoming aware that a one-to-one response is not enough. Structures and systems, perhaps even structures and systems of which we are a part, may oppress the alien, the poor, the widow, and the orphan. The impact of structures may not be apparent. Then oppression may go on silently for years.

Witness this statement of former president Dwight D. Eisenhower, the leader of the Normandy invasion of World War II and the conqueror of Europe. He is speaking of the arms race. Terrifying as it was then, it has ballooned to irrational proportions since then.

> *The worst to be feared and the best to be expected can be simply stated. The worst is atomic war. The best would be this: a life of perpetual fear and tension; a burden of arms draining the wealth and the labor of all people. Every gun that is made, every warship launched, every rocket fired, signifies, in the final sense, a theft from those who hunger and are not fed, those who are cold and are not clothed.*

> *This world in arms is not spending money alone, it is spending the sweat of its laborers, the genius of its science, the hopes of its children.*
>
> *The cost [in 1953 dollars] of one modern heavy bomber is this, a modern brick school in more than thirty cities. It is two electric power plants, each serving a town of sixty thousand in population. It is two fine, fully-equipped hospitals. We pay for a single fighter plane with a half million bushels of wheat. We pay for a single destroyer with new homes that could have housed more than eight thousand people.*
>
> *This is not a way of life at all. Under the cloud of threatening war, it is humanity hanging from a cross of iron.*

Has anything changed in response to this gut-wrenching plea from a man who has experienced the terrors of war firsthand?

Thirty-two years after the Eisenhower statement and forty years to the day of the first atomic device at Los Alamos, New Mexico, five of the major scientists engaged in developing that device came once more to Washington, a constant quest of theirs for these forty years to say to the Congress and President of the United States, "We, who felt the pulse of heat at Trinity [the unusual name for the first atomic device], call on you, our fellow citizens, for a response deep enough to match the insistent signal from the fireball.

"We ask that you join us in insisting on a policy for nuclear weapons that abandons two grand illusions of our times: that nuclear warfare can achieve rational military and political objectives, and that a defense of populations against nuclear attack is possible."

The Eisenhower plea and the five atomic scientists' insistent cry revitalize Zechariah's call to genuine worship: "Thus says the Lord of Hosts, render true judgments, show kindness and mercy each to his brother, do not oppress the widow, the fatherless, the sojourner, or the poor; and let none of you devise evil against his brother in your heart."

If Zechariah's intention needs any further clarity, here is clarity in the person of Jesus Christ. Christ never mistook *forms* of worship for worship, or mistook religious activities for worship. He saw that religion could easily continue while "people could be devising evil in their hearts against their neighbor," the kind that unthinkingly thinks of nuclear winter. For him worship is worship in spirit and in truth, not prescribing and advising, but being and doing and giving and rendering true judgments, showing kindness and mercy, lifting up the widow, the fatherless, the sojourner, the poor; and devising our great good, the good of all in his crucifixion and resurrection. Do we need a more vivid reminder in the day in which we live that we have an infinite capacity to crucify? Do we need to remind ourselves that, because of our infinite capacity to crucify, Christ was willing to be crucified for us that we too might worship in spirit and truth?

That is Christ's deep response, deep enough to match the insistent signal from the fireball of our times. It is that same crucifixion and resurrection which equips us to match the insistent signal from the fireball. It is through that same crucifixion and resurrection that we devise good for the neighbor, not only for the neighbor we know, but for the whole family of God around the world. Amen

For behold, the day comes, burning like an oven, when all the arrogant and all evildoers will be stubble; the day that comes shall burn them up, says the Lord of hosts, so that it will leave them neither root nor branch. But for you who fear my name the sun of righteousness shall rise, with healing in its wings. You shall go forth leaping like calves from the stall. And you shall tread down the wicked, for they will be ashes under the soles of your feet, on the day when I act, says the Lord of hosts.

Remember the law of my servant Moses, the statutes and ordinances that I commanded him at Horeb for all Israel.

Behold, I will send you Elijah the prophet before the great and terrible day of the Lord comes. And he will turn the hearts of fathers to their children and the hearts of children to their fathers, lest I come and smite the land with a curse.

(Malachi 4:1-6)

Malachi 4:1-6   *Proper 28 (C)*
Pentecost 26 (L)
Ordinary Time 33 (RC)

There's Gotta Be a Day

We've heard that song before, haven't we? We've heard it with some variations, but the theme is the same. Perhaps the same problems create the same theme — with some variations. Even the variations do not nuance the repetitions enough to make us pay attention, finally.

If it were not for two things, Malachi's oracle of God could be passed by as "just the same old thing." The oracle is from God. Secondly, it comes because God insists on keeping his covenant. He simply cares. There it is. Do we wish to consider the alternative — a God who does not care?

After reading one prophet after the other, one begins to wonder why the oracle can be so vivid and the response so indifferent. There was little learning, little change.

Perhaps a word would be helpful to respond to that question. The people had returned from exile. Exile was not just "being out of the country." It was a matter of being driven out. Exiles were deprived of their possessions and their sense of place on the land. The response to this loss of a sense of place was lamentations. Exile meant no guarantee of return, ever.

In this instance they had returned with rejoicing. But that had been some years before. They had also begun the rebuilding of the temple, one of their passionate desires. But that had begun years before. Two great moments, they seemed great moments no more.

If the two community preoccupations are no longer preoccupations, what's left? Not surprisingly, the focus now turns to the self. The long-range view isn't paying off, so the short-range view takes over. "What's the use?" takes over. Israel is like the person in quest of some spiritual high which must always be higher than the last. Craving one more mountaintop experience, and finding none to match the last, the seeker begins to lose interest and often sinks below the starting level. So it is with Malachi's people.

There are not many like the former slaves in our country, those who hoped and worked for freedom, decade after decade, even when it became apparent that freedom for this or that one was impossible. There are few like the five atomic scientists who developed, then detonated the first atomic device in Los Alamos, New Mexico. They have been working for forty years since Hiroshima to tell anyone who would listen that it is an illusion that atomic destruction will secure any political or military ends. It is an illusion that the population can be protected against atomic destruction. For them that message has been a forty-year vigil.

Not many of us are like the renowned orchestra conductor, Arturo Toscannini, who rehearsed and performed Beethoven's Ninth Symphony for a lifetime, but would only permit himself to record it when he was eighty. When he was listening to the playback, one person sitting close to him heard him remark, "I think I'm beginning to understand the second movement." In contrast to that, our zeal soon flags. It's hard to be faithful for a few years, much less faithful unto death.

We could conclude from our biblical and personal experience that neither a spiral of goodness nor a spiral of terror changes hearts. One man had a sudden heart attack. He called a pastor, who worked hard to calm him. The young man, in his early thirties, underwent quadruple bypass heart surgery. When the pastor called on him again, he said, "You have much to be thankful for." To that the man — who had been in terror before surgery and was now recuperating well after surgery — said, "I have a strong constitution."

A friend of mine escaped the Communist forces at the end of World War II. She had told herself that she would never complain again if she would only make it to freedom. Then she added, "And here I am, complaining again." The arms race continues over the centuries fed by the belief that the invention of each new weapon will make war so terrible that no one will want to go to war again. The result has been ever more terrible wars, rather than their cessation. Now our weapons are so terrible that to unleash an atomic bomb on the enemy is to unleash that same bomb on ourselves. The very scientists who developed that terror have been unsuccessful in forty years of pleading to get our government to pursue courses other than the multiplication of atomic and hydrogen weapons.

The unrelieved goodness of goods in our nation — and it can be called that when compared to that of other nations — has not really had a better effect on us than that of unrelieved terror. An overall response has been that of the rich man in Christ's story. Confronted by untold wealth and the crisis of storing it all, he said, "I am resolved what to do. I will tear down my barns and build greater." Our largesse has not developed in us a national determination to share that which has been given to us.

I cite these examples — there are more — to help us understand the malaise of response. There needs to be an understanding. But when Malachi has understood it all, when we have understood it all, there is more needed. At its base, the ordinary priests had not done their ordinary jobs, to insure that worship was done properly in the temple. They had grown lax. As a result the people had grown lax. The same was true of people in government. They had grown lax. Corruption had set in. Again, the people, seeing this, had grown lax.

Hence the oracle: All of this will be brought to an end on the day of the Lord. Malachi calls for nothing unusual. He calls for people to be responsive to their responsibilities.

Have you ever realized that there would be no need for heroes if all of us did our common, ordinary, run-of-the-mill duties? The need for giants such as Martin Luther, John Calvin, John Knox, Martin Luther King, Jr., was a response to the failure of the run-of-the-mill priest to do his run-of-the-mill duties.

So Malachi says in effect, "If you would do what you are called to do, there would be no need for an oracle of God. There would be no need for me to deliver it. There would be no need for the day of the Lord which will bring justice to the oppressed, and which will enable the righteous to rejoice like calves running in the spring after being confined all winter.

"The fact is, you have broken your covenant with God. He is your God. You are his people. You have forgotten that, but God has not forgotten. He will not give up on you. You may abandon him, he will not abandon you."

"He calls you to be faithful to the covenant as he is. Why? In times of broken covenant the ones who suffer most are those who can afford to suffer least. That's correct: the widow, the orphan, the alien. And God will not cease caring until these people are given their due because he is the God of all."

Things come apart because we lose a sense of interconnectedness. We are all one family. We are all related. "Hath not one God created us?" asks Malachi. If that is the case, then all of his people are to get what God would like them to have, namely, justice.

You will notice that our Lord talked much the same language as Malachi because the conditions were much the same. He came in the tradition of the prophets. As God had once spoken through the prophets, in these last days He has spoken through His Son. The response to His coming was much the same as the response to the prophets, "If he were killed, no more oracles, no more prophets, no more nuisance." But this last of prophets could not even be silenced by the ridicule of the crucifixion. To a bored, willful people, bored by success, bored by the long haul, bored by the unusual, bored by boredom, the covenant-keeping Son of a covenant-keeping Father said, "Father, forgive them for they know not what they are doing," thereby breaking all the old cycles, whatever they are, and giving us a new day.

And with that he not only points the way, as had many of the prophets, but *became* the way, enabling others to walk that way in the ordinary day, our everyday.

All the tribes of Israel then came to David at Hebron. "Look," they said, "we are your own flesh and blood. In days past when Saul was our king, it was you who led Israel in all their exploits; and Yahweh said to you, 'You are the man who shall be shepherd of my people Israel, you shall be the leader of Israel.' " So all the elders of Israel came to the king at Hebron, and King David made a pact with them at Hebron in the presence of Yahweh, and they anointed David king of Israel. David was thirty years old when he became king, and he reigned for forty years. He reigned in Hebron over Judah for seven years and six months; then he reigned in Jerusalem over all Israel and Judah for thirty-three years.

(2 Samuel 5:1-5)

2 Samuel 5:1-5 — Christ the King

Whoever Would Be King

The path to David's coronation did not run as smoothly as this passage may indicate. His succession was nothing like the transition from King George VI to the present Queen Elizabeth. Despite the fact that God had anointed David king, that anointing preceded this one of the text by quite some time. Blood was shed, more than we like to remember — some by David, though he was careful never to lay his hand on God's anointed, his predecessor Saul, but much of the slaughter was by David's lieutenants.

Despite the fact that King David became one of the outstanding symbols — to be like David was to be like the Lord's anointed, messianic — the Scriptures do not glamorize his kingship. Saul's failures, David's weaknesses, and the sins of his successors fill the Scriptural accounts. Alongside his wisdom Solomon had an exploitative nature which hastened the downfall of both kingdoms ultimately. Solomon furthered slavery and accumulated enormous wealth in the capital city.

God had warned the people about the danger of having their own king. A king's charter is the welfare of the citizens. Most kings quickly alter the charter to make themselves their first concern, the beneficiaries of their own welfare. People serve kings rather than kings people. David was not exempt from this. Uriah and Bathsheba and Absolom shall forever be linked with his name along with his psalms. Even as David died, the borders which he had enlarged were not Israel's beyond dispute. At its height, David's kingdom was a pattern of fragility, a fragility marked by fraternal strife between the northern and southern parts of the kingdom, which led to a final dissolution of the kingdom forever, after the reign of Solomon.

But for a moment, fleeting as it was, in David there was a glimpse of the beginning of a realization of what might be possible. Messianic vision clarified and strengthened itself through his kingship. And that Davidic symbol carried the hopes, the dreams, down throughout history, until one who was more David than David, the mature David, the David of God's dream, rested on the throne.

The second David sought to unite not only all of Israel, but the whole world. And just as the people of David's time fought against their being included, so did the people of Christ's time, and so do we at the present time. And, as Israel paid a heavy price for its fraternal strife, so do we all. Differences and diversity, given as gifts for enrichment, are often the basis for divisions. The wealth of differences between races and cultures soon degenerates into poverty of ridicule. Theoretical equality may be a sometime word in our vocabulary. In actual practice, the law — not belief — enforces an outward semblance of equality and unity.

Christ insisted on a loss of distinctions among people. The righteous need him as much as the unrighteous; the rich as much as the poor; the strong as much as the weak; the people within Israel as much as those outside of Israel. All need all, all the time. For all of that; Christ's radical innovation seemed as fragile as the unity of the Israel of David and Solomon.

How can the best and the worst be lumped together? Do you mean to say that no one is automatically advantaged or disadvantaged? Christ's answer was (is), "No!"

We continue to say, "No," to *his*, "No!" for the most part today. That the evidence is clear, now more than ever, that we are one family, matters nothing.

We live from each other, says Charles Williams. We live from whomever. We sing and play music that's been composed some hundreds of years in the past. We read books written, in some cases, thousands of years ago. Most of us have been freed from polio and its effects through the work of Dr. Jonas Salk. We live from food harvested, in some cases, from farms and orchards on the other side of the planet.

One person's clothing on a given day may well testify to the world's unity: he owes a debt to France by his shirt, Ireland by his necktie, Yugoslavia by his coat, Poland by his trousers, Germany by his overcoat, Spain by his shoes, Italy by his belt. His stereo is made in Japan, his camera in Hong Kong, his dinnerware in Red China. If he wears spectacles, they are a likely product of OPEC oil.

The story could go on. The point is, we are indissolubly connected with each other. Despite our American doctrine of "Man As Master," of independence, we are, at our core, as dependent as all others. So dependent are we that we even live off our enemies. Many in the West eat three meals a day because the West is hostile to Russia. Many in Russia eat because of their hostility to Americans. Each engages in making arms against the other.

If by nothing else, a spiral of global terror unites us. If nothing else, our common need for oxygen unites us. When there is no oxygen we die. We all eat. We all drink. Even such basic universal necessities do not bring us together because even such unity is not recognized.

When David became king of all Israel, he was not creating a new family any more than do rival countries by signing a peace treaty. David's kingship was only recognizing that which already was. But given his conditions and our conditions, recognizing that which *is* takes some doing.

In the midst of all this, why bother with Christ's kingship? He seems to be weakness incorporated. How we despise weakness! He hardly seems the fulfillment of "that day," repeatedly prophesied as a threat or encouragement throughout Hebrew history. But Christ claimed that day, "I have come to announce the acceptable year of the Lord." And when he sat down, he said, "This day this saying has been fulfilled in your hearing." (Luke 4)

What was that day in all of its fullness? Contrast David and Christ for some clarity. David rose from an obscure shepherd boy to king, from youngest in his family to first in the nation. Jesus put aside his own greatness, pursued the route of downward mobility, emptied himself, took our form and shape, and became obedient to death, even the death of a criminal. Christ went from the heights to the depths, from glory to degradation. His humiliation was his coronation, reputation destroyed, family intimidated, friends scattered. In contrast to David's prestigious court, Christ had self-confessed thieves in the regal setting of a crucifixion. All the tribes of Israel gathered at Hebron to proclaim David's kingship. At the cross there were two women and one man. A thief and a captain of the guard recognized some kingly qualities in Christ.

Two more contrasting coronations could not have been planned. Crucifixions, of course, are not prime P.R. material. But there was much more at stake here than a P.R. venture. Kings ignore those whom they wish. Not this king. His every action was for people. And Christ's being for people is, for many, as repulsive as his crucifixion. In fact, one can say that care for people, for all people, was that which brought on his crucifixion. To care for all people is to revolutionize the way we live. The original crucifixion recognized that. We still do. Not only society, but the church, too, often resists and even justifies "including people out."

This king has a radical solidarity with us. Not based on arms, or intimidation, or bribery, or even conviviality, his solidarity with us is rooted in his being one of us. That's a new way for kings. Many a king or president professes love for the people, but the press and history tell us more than one monarch has robbed the very people professed to be loved. Not this king. Run-of-the-mill kings are given to killing folks. This king is given to dying for folks, a contrast even now not yet fully appreciated.

What's the kingdom of this new king like? We've already said much. The kingdom is like the king. He is determined to turn the image of king upsidedown. Kings are to serve, not be served. This king does his Father's will, not only in heaven but also on earth. Life is about doing the Father's will.

This king creates a new starting point, a new point of view, a new way of looking at things. This king gives new lenses. In the words of Bornkamm, "Redemption now means 'change of rulers,' liberation from the tyrannies of the powers of the world. But still more: it means liberation to obey him who himself was obedient and has become Lord and Victor."

In a marvelous way God now enlists us to establish his righteousness. And why not? "God meets man who wants to be as God by wanting to be nothing other than a man. The lordship of this one is freedom. But this means at the same time humiliation and obedience are now henceforth the kingly way of faith . . ." (Bornkamm)

Sounds like a dream this king is dreaming. But the dream sounds like a real dream. And it is his dream for our everyday. Let all say, "Jesus Christ is Lord. Jesus Christ is King to the glory of God the Father. Amen"

The time is coming, says the Lord, when I will make a new covenant with Israel and Judah. It will not be like the covenant I made with their forefathers when I took them by the hand and led them out of Egypt. Although they broke my covenant, I was patient with them, says the Lord. But this is the covenant which I will make with Israel after those days, says the Lord; I will set my law within them and write it on their hearts; I will become their God and they shall become my people. No longer need they teach one another to know the Lord; all of them, high and low alike, shall know me, says the Lord, for I will forgive their wrongdoing and remember their sin no more.

(Jeremiah 31:31-34)

Jeremiah 31:31-34   *Reformation Sunday*

The Time Is Coming

This prophecy does not have the sound and fury of many another. Here is a sweet, gentle breeze, refreshing, invigorating. Jeremiah in his own person is much like the tone of this prophecy. If you've read much of Jeremiah, it may surprise you to learn that he was of a shy, gentle disposition. He wanted people about him. He was affectionate. In this prophecy he is talking about a new law God will write in the heart. Spontaneity of obedience will come from deep inside rather than being imposed from the outside. Jeremiah had some experience with this imposition of the law from the outside. There's a kind of slam-bang character about his prophecies that are in sharp contrast to his personality. The harshness of the prophecies — never mind their truth — drove away his friends, alienated his family, embroiled him with the government, entangled him with the priests. It culminated in his exile and a death unknown.

Not the least to be alienated was Jeremiah himself. So bitter did he become that he cried out that God had seduced him, had raped him, and forced him to be a prophet against his will. Once he deliberately refused to prophesy because it was tearing him apart, but so also did silence. "A fire was burning within my heart, imprisoned in my bones, the effort to repress it wearied me. I could not bear it." Jeremiah wished he had never been born. He would have preferred an announcement of his abortion to that of his birth. Contrary to everything he felt and desired, Jeremiah had to say he was chosen to be a prophet before he was born and that God had stitched him together in his mother's womb with all the care of a professional seamstress.

Such was the nature of true prophecy that the prophet had no choice but to say what God had asked him to say. Whether he wanted to speak or not, so he must speak. It seemed to be of no concern, at least to God, that he asked a prophet to speak in ways out of harmony with his personality. Let shy, sensitive Jeremiah say and think what he will, God has him speak harshly over a longer period of time than almost any other prophet. To know how shocking that is, place it against our culture's virtual adoration of harmony of the integrated personality.

A man of some wealth, Jeremiah lived a life of renunciation and self-denial. Altogether, it could be said about him as it could be said about most prophets, "They are wonderful in heaven. They are hell on earth." That could also be said about Martin Luther, whose moment is celebrated this Reformation Sunday. It's marvelous to have Luther as a hero some five hundred years later. How many of us would have been happy to have lived at his time or to have lived with him, I'm not sure. Prophets are a driven people, driven by none other than God himself. We are not used to their kind of certainty, nor an accountability which answers to God alone and is beholden to none among people.

But today's text lets it be known that the prophet is not always talking tough. Yet the fulfillment of today's splendid text seems no nearer realization than did the fulfillment of the slam-bang prophecies seem to be when all was well. The good seems no more likely of realization than the destructive. But there the prophecy stands, all the more powerful and persuasive because this prophecy comes from the mouth of someone whose prophecies were not usually shaped by the gentle and sublime.

This new law, placed in the heart, creates a response arising from an inward spontaneity and obedience, rather than having been imposed from the outside by the prophet's constant hammering and threatening. To us this may not be revolutionary because we "have a thing about" sincerity and interiorizing, of genuineness and integrity, of personal responsibility. But for the people of Jeremiah's time? Since the beginning, prophet after prophet calls them to keep their covenant with Jahweh. Now all that was to stop. It would stop because it was no longer necessary: God would put his law within them. He would write it in their hearts. No one would any longer need to teach another. No one would have to be instructed by the other. Could that be possible? All of those other prophecies no longer necessary? No repeats? No re-runs? What a day that would be indeed!

And not only for them, but for us. Our immediate history may not be a parallel to that of Jeremiah's people, but it's closer than we realize. Can the promise hold for us as well? No one needs to tell us anymore? No one needs to teach us anymore? What about war? We come some years after Jeremiah. We still have to learn. Someone still has to teach us that killing people as a national or international policy solves no problems. We are now prepared to prove that, in a strange way, by the overdevelopment of some fifty thousand nuclear devices. The firepower of one nuclear submarine exceeds all the bombs dropped in World War I and World War II by a factor of seven.

We don't have to be taught anymore? We have known for many years that there's enough food for everybody. Except for sporadic efforts, there has been no sustained action to carry out what we know we are able to do.

We don't have to be taught anymore? Life does not consist of the things that we possess, yet Western culture encourages ruthless acquisition of more. "More," not measured by any standard except that there's always room for more. Since this cannot be measured, the lust for more continues without hindrance. We have a habit of thinking we can make something of ourselves by seizing things outside of ourselves."

And as to remembering, someone once said that we learn all that we learn by the time we are two. From that time on, we always have to be reminded. Parents know that. How often, contrary to the prophecy, must they tell their children to pick up, to do this, to do that? Then, upon the child's graduation from college at the ripe age of twenty-two, parental reminding continues, needs to continue.

But for all that, few deny their preference for God's new covenant. Falling in love, being in love is something like that new vision. Perhaps you've experienced it. When you first fell in love, neither of the two of you needed instruction. You both knew in your heart what any particular moment needed. You both knew the desire and the need of the other and responded immediately. No one looks to that time as a bad time or a sad time. Everyone laments the passage of that time. Everyone longs for the return of that moment of experienced reality, the way things really ought to be. If the world were right, that is the way it would be — not for *some* moments, but for *all* moments in all times and in all places.

I'm puzzled by the derision heaped on "people being in love," as though that were not genuine. Some prefer, it would seem, harshness, cruelty, lack of common courtesy and civility. Our pop stars may sing of being in love too much. We sing of it too little.

Take the instance of people falling in love — knowing what they ought to do without being taught and responding the way they know they ought — take that and multiply it a thousand times. Then you capture the beginning of the vastness of the radicality of Jeremiah's prophecy. Add to that the fact that this prophecy is for everybody, "for low and high alike." Utopian dreams are commonly dreamt for an exclusive group. The dream hinges on the exclusive. Thus, the Utopian dream incorporates the problems of the old dream, its need for the exclusive.

Not so here. This is for all. It eliminates the prestigious difference, the lust for the exclusive. How much do we experience that which is applicable for all? Those who breathe, those who face death, are all included.

What's new in this new vision? It sounds too good to be true. What's the trick and the treat? The vision is powerful, yet its power can be easily lost. "No longer need they teach one another to know the Lord; all of them, high and low alike, shall know me, says the Lord, for I will forgive their wrongdoing and remember their sin no more."

They shall all know *me*; that is, know what I stand for, what I am like, what I desire, what my dreams are, what I intend toward people, what I have done and am willing to do, to know me as the giver God, whose delight it is to give his creatures all things, as witnessed to by the creation, one who, despite the disobedience of people, still has not abandoned his covenant, "I shall be your God and you shall be my people." The power behind the vision is nothing less than God himself.

I will forgive them their wrongdoing and remember their sin no more. "Since it has become obvious that you cannot come to me, I shall come to you." How radical! The usual response to failure is punishment. Not so with this God. This God comes to the one who has failed. He comes all the way. That's what forgiveness means — coming all the way to those who are not able, because of their own fault, to come any of the way. I will forgive their wrongdoing. Is that any way to deal with wrongdoing? Will not wrongdoing thereby be multiplied? I will remember their sin no more. That is, their relationship will no longer be governed by their failure to respond to me. After this their relationship will be governed by my not remembering. My memory will be that of forgiveness rather than the memory of the depth of their sin.

What kind of God would do that? That is simply God. Paul's language is much like that of Jeremiah. God acquits the *guilty!* But aren't the *innocent* acquitted, and not the *guilty?* Not so in *this* covenant. Did sin abound? Then did grace much *more* abound. No one else deals that way, only this God.

From the Second Lesson for this day: "Quite independently of the law, God's justice has been brought to light. The law and the prophets both bear witness to it; it is God's way of righting wrong. It is effective through faith in Christ for all who have such faith — all, without distinction. For all alike have sinned, and are deprived of the divine splendor, and all are justified by God's free grace alone, through his act of liberation in the person of Christ Jesus. For God designed him to be the means of expiating sin by his sacrificial death, effective through faith. God meant by this to demonstrate his justice because in his forbearance he had overlooked the sins of the past — to demonstrate his justice now in the present, showing that He is Himself just and also justifies any man who puts his faith in Jesus." Breathtaking!

God demonstrates his justice, God proves that he is just, by justifying those who have faith in Christ Jesus. His way of righting our wrongs is not by getting us to right them, because we could not, but righting them through Christ Jesus.

The poignancy of Christ sharing the cup at the Last Supper! "This is the blood of the new covenant shed for you. Do this in remembrance of me." Do you see and feel the accent? Christ, who forgives, has the accent; not our sin. Kierkegaard prayed, "Lord, teach us to remember not how much we have sinned, but rather how much thou hast forgiven." Yes, it takes the blood of the covenant to do it. The Eucharist will not let us forget. Without the shedding of blood there is no forgiveness. Mysteriously, someone pays. God pays. That's the new covenant in the blood of the Son of God. Jeremiah could not possibly have dreamed all that he dreamt.

But there is a sobering note. Some careful students of the New Testament say that the later writings in the New Testament begin to reflect a belief in the ineffectiveness of God's forgiveness, this freedom spoken of so vividly in the Epistle to the Galatians. It is subtle, to be sure, but hints of added rules and regulations begin to appear. Paul saw and tasted and preached this magnificence, but he had to take the Galatians to task: "Why have you turned to another gospel?" Luther saw and tasted and preached this magnificence, but before he died he lamented that it did not seem to work. Kierkegaard was critical of the church of his time because of its blase attitude toward the God who would remember their sin no more.

Perhaps we, too, can easily forget the power of the resurrected life that is ours, the power of a God who forgives our iniquities and remember our sin no longer. A man was once complaining about his lot in life. A friend recalled a long series of blessings that God had given him. To that the other replied, "Yes, but that was yesterday. What has he done for me today?" It is well to remember that the lust for the security of the brick yards of Egypt can all too readily quickly outweigh the promise of the wilderness.

Grace does not lose its touch, but we can all too readily lose our touch with grace and find ourselves back in the days before Jeremiah's brilliant vision, clinging to the days of rules and regulations rather than a heart that has been renewed, a heart that no longer needs to be taught.

The festival of the Reformation, the celebration of this Reformation Sunday recalls not only this prophecy of Jeremiah, not only the complete fulfillment of the prophecy in the life and the crucifixion and the death of the resurrected Christ. It recalls not only the "new covenant in my blood" of the Holy Supper. It recalls not only a high moment in the life of Martin Luther. It calls us all once more to the brilliant dream that God dreamt into reality in the life of his Son, the dream he still loves to dream, to teach us that which no longer needs to be taught, to tell us that which no longer needs to be told by planting deep within our musculature, our nervous system, our bloodstream: that he is our God and that we are his people, because he forgives us our iniquity and remembers our sin no more. Amen

In the first year of Belshazzar, king of Babylon, as Daniel lay on his bed, dreams and visions came into his head. Then he wrote down the dream, and here his account begins:

In my visions of the night I, Daniel, was gazing intently and I saw a great sea churned up by the four winds of heaven, and four huge beasts coming up out of the sea, each one different from the others.

My spirit within me was troubled, and, dismayed by the visions which came into my head, I, Daniel, approached one of those who stood there and inquired from him what all this meant; and he told me the interpretation. "These great beasts, four in number," he said, "are four kingdoms which shall rise from the ground. But the saints of the Most High shall receive the kingly power and shall retain it for ever, for ever and ever."

(Daniel 7:1-3, 15-18)

Daniel 7:1-3, 15-18   *All Saints' Sunday*

Beasts, Saints and Chaos

"But the saints of the Most High shall receive the kingly power and shall retain it for ever, for ever and ever." But we are not there yet; neither were the people of the text. Because they were not yet there and we are not yet there, we gather here to reflect that some are already there but the rest of us are not yet there.

We have enough trouble without the troublesome word "saint" — "the saints of the Most High shall receive the kingly power and shall retain it for ever, for ever and ever." "But I'm no saint," someone will say. Another, "But remember that still does not make me a saint."

"Saint" makes us nervous. That anyone would think of us as saints? Some pastors believe their task is to show that they are not saints. I did not think that required a personal campaign. Two weeks scrutiny of any one of us would make that clear.

We sometimes associate an exclusiveness with the word "saint." Perfection, we mean. Even the proud are reluctant to associate perfection with their name or reputation, at least to say so themselves. No matter how common is the misunderstanding of saint, the Scriptures do not so misunderstand it. In his epistles, Paul addresses the members of the congregations as saints, people called as saints; notice, not just to be and become saints, but they are saints even as he addresses them. Even the congregation at Corinth, guilty of a most grievous sin, continuing in that sin even as Paul writes, he addresses as saints.

Do we need more evidence? The list of heroic saints in the eleventh chapter of Hebrews is not ours: Noah, who got drunk at the end of the ark trip; Abraham, to save his life once denied that Sarah was his wife; Isaac, who botched the blessing of his son; Jacob, whose very name means deception; Moses, who was both reluctant to be God's servant and then who killed because he misunderstood what he was to be; Rahab, one of Christ's ancestors, was a prostitute; and of David and Samson I need not tell you.

Whatever else the word "saint" may mean to us, in the Scriptures it does not mean perfect, without flaw. Nor does it carry the image of soft but ineffectual; pleasant but unrealistic; good humored but not tough in the clinches. The book of Daniel is not hesitant to use the term *saint* because it knows what saint means.

"Saints" mean the holy ones of God. Holiness is not an achievement. It is the gift of God himself. Holiness is a gift, notice, not a reward or an award. It is a gift that God first gave baptized ones in our baptism. In baptism he incorporated us into himself and all that he is, all that he means. Our holiness is the gift of the generosity of his Son's death and resurrection. The old hymn says, "Jesus thy blood and thy righteousness, they are my beauty, my glorious dress." Our holiness is the cloak of another. We are made holy by another.

That helps in times of persecution, as was the case at the time of this writing. There was a persecution led by Antiochus Epiphanes. By telling of the resistance, persistance, and the perseverance of people like Daniel and others during one persecution, the writer wants to encourage the people of the present in their perseverance and in their persistence. If others stood up, that should help them stand up.

While Daniel is a person of some heroic proportions, the Festival of All Saints recalls all in the past who persisted and all in the present who do persist.

If the truth be known, the mere recitation of heroes of faith may *dis*courage rather than *en*courage. "If only the heroes can make it, I can't make it because I'm no hero." All Saints is for the encouragement of the entire church, heroic and non-heroic members of it alike.

C. S. Lewis in his book, *The Great Divorce,* illuminates how holiness and sainthood have to do with the common and ordinary and everyday Christian, the non-heroic as well as the heroic. People are touring heaven to get a feel of what it is like before making a choice to stay or not to stay. As the tour proceeds, suddenly music fills the air. Lights are dazzling. A parade is underway.

"For whom?" inquires a tourist. "For a general?" answering her own question. (We just love our wars.)

"No," is the answer.

"For an artist?" (There are times when we venerate our artists.)

"No." Again the reply.

"Ah, I should have known. It's for a bishop."

"Most certainly not," is the reply. "Your own experience should have told you that. It's for Mrs. Smith of Golders Green."

"Why for her?"

"Because for an entire lifetime she loved her husband and her cat." (And if you know anything about husbands and cats . . .)

An insignificant woman doing the insignificant, but no less holy, no less saint for all that. Martin Luther said that everything from the work of a woman scrubbing a floor to a preacher preaching the gospel becomes a holy action as it is or is not done to the glory of God.

In fact, one of our temptations fed by our culture is that of making the heroic a substitute for the persistent in the ordinary. Almost any person at a given moment is capable of doing the heroic. Recall the men who raised the flag on Mount Surabachi in World War II, an action commemorated in history books and with a postage stamp. Their Mount Surabachi moment was followed by sadness and deep disappointment.

Sometimes the early church made a similar mistake. Heroes of faith were on occasion made bishops, a task for which they were unequal. The steady kind of courage of a Mrs. Smith of Golders Green is a courage which the church needs more of. The special, the unusual, the extraordinary is so highlighted by the world and sometimes by the church that the more needed is too little encouraged. For most of us the temptation of being insignificant, of not making a difference, of not counting for something is strong because that indeed describes most of us.

The passage of time, too, is a great trial for many. The fact that Monday follows Sunday and keeps on following Sunday; for some, eighty years; for some, ninety years, is a greater trial than a dramatic confrontation with an athiest. That is why we hear, "Be faithful unto death." That is why, "Do not grow weary in well-doing." If what we are doing is well, then we are to keep on doing it. You notice that weariness, which is much in our minds, is not at all in the mind of the writer. Instantaneity is our thing, not patience.

This sense of weariness and loss of a sense of worthwhileness is compounded by a sense of isolation. "I, only I in all of Israel have not bowed the knee to Baal," is the immortal expression of Elijah, who has spoken for all of us at one time or another. Our culture, often the church, promotes that sense of isolation with its excessive stress on individualism, of making it on one's own, of failing on one's own, of everything good and bad revolving around the self. The self is a shaky reed at best. Luther's words, "We pray that the devil, the world, and our flesh may not deceive us or seduce us into misbelief, despair and other . . ." When the focus is on the self, the indicator on the dial vacillates between pride and despair. "I don't need anybody or anything," or "Nobody or nothing can be of any help."

How we perceive temptation may determine how we weather it. If God is to help, he needs to remove the circumstances which cause the pain. Such action, and *only* such action, will mean that he is of any help. And that, of course, is one possibility. There is another: to pray for a double measure of strength to bear the load.

The vision of the Daniel text is the latter: the vision of the sea of chaos, the four beasts ready to devour people. But it's not the beasts, nor the chaos but the saints of the King who will reign for ever and ever. Christ vivifies everything. Could I not call twelve legions of angels? Remember, the moment of the crucifixion then was not seen as the moment of triumph we see it to be now. There was the onslaught of the government, of religion, of the military, of the common people, the desertion of disciples, and at last the desertion by his Father. It may be light now, but then it was darkness. Even though the darkness may not always be dispelled, Christ gives light and is the light in the midst of that darkness. He gives us the courage to enter the most negative experiences with hope.

Daniel, confident and courageous, enters the lion's den; Shadrach, Meshach and Abednego, confident and courageous, defy a ruthless ruler and enter the burning fiery furnace, not as victims but as kings. They knew they were not alone, no matter how alone they appeared to be.

And that is always the case. We are not alone. It was true of Dietrich Bonhoeffer and Martin Luther King, Jr., and Pastor Hernandez, and Bishop Romero who was assassinated as he celebrated the Eucharist. It is true for Bishop Desmond Tutu and Dean T. Simon Farisani and Pastor Gomez. No matter how much the government and the police try to isolate and intimidate and torture, their intended victims are not alone. They are accompanied. Someone has gone that way before.

Perhaps our self-doubts about our faithfulness are doubts about

God's faithfulness. Look at history. God encouraged us, I was with Daniel and Shadrach and Meshach and Abednego. If I was faithful then, will I not be faithful now? I was with James and Peter and John. If I was faithful then, will I not be faithful now? I was with the Luthers and the Calvins and the Bonhoeffers. If I was faithful then, will I not also be faithful to you? I am with the Desmond Tutus and the Simon Farisanis and the Gomezes, the African Christians often dying these days by the score. If I am with them, am I not also with you, not only now but into your future?

More than that. He feeds us now as he has always fed us with the body and blood of his Son in the Holy Supper. Chaos and violence threatened Christ on every side and in every moment. This most holy meal, this most holy moment is beset by violence and the language of violence. In the night in which he was betrayed, he without whom nothing was made that was made; in the night in which he was betrayed by violence into violence which ruthlessly violated him and the world he had created; in that night of betrayal when we could have expected him to do anything but what he did do, he took bread and blessed it and broke it and gave it to his disciples and said, "This is my body broken for you. Do this in remembrance of me." Then after supper when he had given thanks, he took the cup and said, "This is the new covenant in my blood. Drink of it; all of you. Do this as often as you drink it in remembrance of me."

By that action, and the action of submitting to his flogging — until the bones on his back and ribs showed their white — his being jeered, his being stripped naked, his being made to carry the cross, then the nailing of his hands and feet to the cross until his humiliation became his coronation, he made clear that he would be with us to the end and beyond. I am with you. "They may kill you but they can't touch you. Were you to take the wings of the morning and fly to the uttermost parts of the earth or descend deep into the abyss, I will be with you."

He will be with us here and now in our time. For it is here that his name is to be hallowed; it is here that his kingdom is to come; it is here that his will is to be done on earth, the same earth where he originated that prayer.

Christ gives us himself through the common, ordinary bread and wine, through the common, ordinary means of eating and drinking. We eat and drink together to experience his presence not only in the meal but in each other. If he makes his presence felt in the gift of himself in the unspectacular, he most certainly will make himself felt in the spectacular. And he promises to feed us this meal as long as we draw breath.

Oh, the vision sees the chaos. It sees the four avaracious and malicious beasts, but it says, "The saints of the Most High shall receive the kingly power and shall retain it for ever, for ever and ever."

And with a twinkle in his eyes, the Lord says, "The last time I checked, you had not yet resisted the shedding of your own blood," there's still some space for that. Amen

"When you come into the land which the Lord your God gives you for an inheritance, and have taken possession of it, and live in it, you shall take some of the first of all the fruit of the ground, which you harvest from your land that the Lord your God gives you, and you shall put it in a basket, and you shall go to the place which the Lord your God will choose, to make his name to dwell there. And you shall go to the priest who is in office at that time, and say to him, 'I declare this day to the Lord your God that I have come into the land which the Lord swore to our fathers to give us.' Then the priest shall take the basket from your hand and set it down before the altar of the Lord your God.

"And you shall make response before the Lord your God, 'A wandering Aramean was my father; and he went down into Egypt and sojourned there, few in number; and there he became a nation, great, mighty, and populous. And the Egyptians treated us harshly, and afflicted us, and laid upon us hard bondage. Then we cried to the Lord the God of our fathers, and the Lord heard our voice, and saw our affliction, our toil, and our oppression; and the Lord brought us out of Egypt with a mighty hand and an outstretched arm, with great terror, with signs and wonders; and he brought us into this place and gave us this land, a land flowing with milk and honey. And behold, now I bring the first of the fruit of the ground, which thou, O Lord, hast given me.' And you shall set it down before the Lord your God, and worship before the Lord your God; and you shall rejoice in all the good which the Lord your God has given to you and to your house, you, and the Levite, and the sojourner who is among you."

(Deuteronomy 26:1-11)

Deuteronomy 26:1-11   *Thanksgiving Eve/Thanksgiving Day*

To Thank Is To . . .

This ritual of Thanksgiving is a ritual of identification. A traditional American parade ritualizes the sacredness and centeredness of money in American life.

This Deuteronomic ritual identifies God as the center of thanksgiving and is our way of saying so. One does not thank anybody if self is the center. Thanks, then, may be little more than the oil of social facilitation. The thanksgiving of this text expresses a relationship of debt. It calls forth one's history — not of one's lifetime alone, but that of all previous generations.

Once the Israelites came to the land that God had promised to give them, they were called to remember that their ancestors were once homeless, that they became powerful in Egypt, that they were humiliated and ill-treated, suffered all kinds of cruelty, even the cruelty of slavery. Then God brought them out of Egypt with a mighty hand and a stretched-out arm. They were to recall and recite out loud all of this history as they brought their gifts of tithe.

Note how the accent is not on the people's *destitution* but God's *restitution*. They are because he is. Note also in this text that, despite the wanderings, the wars, the privations, the hard work of the people, this passage accents "the first fruits of the land I *have given* you; when you have entered into the land which I *have given* you; he brought to us this place and *gave* us this land; the first fruits, O Lord, which you *have given* me; all the good things which the Lord *has given*."

The text identifies them as receivers, not because of merit, but because it is God's nature to give himself richly. After all that God had given them, must he still remind them to give thanks? Much of the Old Testament history is a history of their thanklessness, their indifference, and self-satisfaction, especially in moments of great affluence when one would think they would remember God most — but when they remembered him least.

Isn't that much of our own personal and national history? Because we happen to live in a country (reflect on that word "happen" for a moment) which is rich in soil, in mountains, in forests, we think somehow that we produced it all. We heap thanksgiving on ourselves rather than God. If we respond that our minds and our hard work have done all this, we have only to ask, "Who is the source of our minds? Who is the source of our energy? Who is the source of our ingenuity?" We recognize quickly that it is all God's gift, no matter how you cut it.

It is hard to recognize God as the giver in a culture which praises the "self-made woman" and "self-made man" as national achievements, who cheer people who make their first million before they are thirty, who laud people who achieve mastery, as though mastery were ever a solo job; who laud people who dominate others and carry out that domination internationally through the ruthless exertion of our national and industrial powers on others, regardless of the price we make them pay for our exploitation; in a country where to be number one is the highest accolade. How then do we realize that the source of it all is none other than the giver God?

Moreover, the necessity and the felt need for thanksgiving is harder come by for us than for the Dueteronomic Israelite. We are, most of us, at some experiential distance from the ritual of seed, root, stem, leaf, and fruit. It comes to most of us through stores, in cartons and packages, not on stalks of grain, not in the udders of cows. Joseph Sittler highlights this dilemma. A modern man "crouches over levers of a crane and guides it to lift stone from Indiana, which he has never touched, to the top of a construction job in Omaha, where it is fixed in walls he need not look at, designed for purposes he has nothing to do with, by men whose names he does not know and whose faces he never sees."

It is difficult, then, to have a sense of dependence that is the lifeblood of thanksgiving. When we calculate all we have been given, we easily bypass the essentials highlighted in Luther's explanation of the first article of the Creed: "I believe that God has made me and all creatures; that He has given me my body and soul, eyes, ears, and all my members, my reason and all my senses, and still preserves them; also clothing and shoes, meat and drink, house and home, wife and children, fields, and cattle and all my goods; that he richly and daily provides me with all that I need to support this body and life; that he defends me against all danger, and guards and protects me from all evil; and all this out of purely fatherly divine goodness and mercy, without any merit or worthiness in me."

The experience of the crane operator is at some remove from Martin's. That of the computer analyst, and that of the 747 jet pilot are even more so. While one would think that the new complexity would heighten the sense of thanksgiving because of the wonder and amazement of it all, more often than not it actually results in boredom. Grade school children are bored. High school children are bored. College students are bored. My own children never bring up the subject of the wonder of traveling across the skies at speeds upwards of four hundred miles an hour. They have all traveled much. They are all quite unimpressed.

Boredom is a far cry from the attitude of the text. Boredom is a far cry from Martin Luther's "for all of which I am in God's debt to thank and to praise, to serve and obey Him." In his debt just by being born, just being born puts us in a posture of praise and thanksgiving. In a country which has so many people who have so much, we find it hard to believe it is not really ours, never has been, never will be in any possessive sense. Even the tithe in the text has been distorted to mean God's share. "Once we have given God his share, then we free to do with the rest as we please," the common thinking runs. In truth there is no such thing as "God's share" or "my share." There is only God's. Whether the funds feed the poor or buy me a double dip, chocolate mint ice cream sugar cone, the funds remain God's. The few moments funds are in my hands doesn't change that. There's a fierce kind of scriptural logic about that. "For we brought nothing into this world and we certainly shall carry nothing out." When Nelson Rockerfeller's daughter saw her father in his coffin, she remarked, "He looks so small." To that the pastor said, "None of us is larger than life-size."

The sheer "is-ness" of our relationship to a giver God calls for a "free and glad recognition of our indebtedness to him." The free and glad recognition of lovers' indebtedness to each other, multiplied many times over, gives us some grasp of the vastness of our indebtedness to God. Lovers know they are in each other's debt. What is more, they freely and gladly recognize the debt. Their indebtedness evokes sheer adoration of the other. Their sheer pleasure is endless because their debt is limitless. So it is with their love, knowing no bounds. "It is forbidden," says the Talmud, "to taste of this world without saying a blessing."

This kind of adoration and thanksgiving is not part of our everyday world. "If civilization sobered up for two days would it not die on the third of remorse?" asks Malcolm Lowery.

Thanksgiving is not optional. Thanksgiving grows out of the heart and guts of our identity. We have received the richest of His gifts. God made us what we are, formed us in our mothers wombs. God is forever giving us the first fruits — himself. He never ceases in his giving of first fruits — his Son.

As God detailed his Deuteronomic gift of himself, in that same detail he insinuated Christ into our life. He wove the fabric so closely that our destiny became his destiny. He was thankful as we are thankless. He was crucified because we have an infinite capacity to crucify. He was killed because we are killers. He died, for to be one of us is to die. It is our destiny. And now he has become the first fruits of the resurrection.

We were not there for that specifically, but no matter. God continues to give. He gives his Son to us in baptism where we become what he is because he became what we are. Now we are prime examples of the way God rights wrongs. That means life for us on a new plane altogether.

In the Lord's Supper he gives us the first fruits again, the body and blood of his Son. This covenant is the new covenant in the blood of Christ, the Son of God. This is not a tithe or even tithes. God is giving us totally God. He does this that we might remember the Christ, our life's blood. This remembering is not a test of memory recall. It is a healing of a relationship that has been marred or broken. It is the restoration of his presence. It is new life. The Supper identifies God as the One who died for us and rose again. The Holy Supper identifies us. We are people who had to be died for. That he gives himself to us in the death and resurrection of his Son is our new land. That is the land to which God has led us and which he has given us. He is our new country. No land is like that land.

We come to him as receivers, cupped hands held high, mouths open to receive gifts of life, the gift of God. Luther bluntly calls us "beggars before God." No matter who we are, no matter what our achievements, we are beggars before God.

And when beggars eat, that calls for rejoicing. We celebrate the Sacrament. We joy in the Eucharist as God's giving of himself over and over again, as God once more reaches down with a mighty hand and a stretched-out arm with signs and wonders and gives us new life, a life flowing with milk and honey.

If the meal of milk and honey is for beggars, all are included. Rejoicing is neither selective nor restrictive. As we receive, so we give. Rejoicing spills out over everybody and is *for* everybody — the stranger, the alien, because "your fathers were once slaves in Egypt. It was impossible for them to rescue themselves, "but I brought you out with a strong hand and an outstretched arm; therefore be hospitable to slaves; you were once a stranger in a strange land, therefore be hospitable to strangers.

Robert MacAfee Brown says, "When in the Lord's Supper we eat and drink the body and blood of Christ, it unites us with all others who eat and drink the body and blood of Christ. And it unites us with all others who eat and drink. And last, but not least, it unites us with all others who would eat if they only had something to eat, who would drink if they only had something to drink."

United with all others by this feast, we serve all others. May the day of the Thanksgiving turkey and the Christmas basket and the Easter ham never pass. But we need to pass beyond them all. I believe it was Matthew Fox who said, "I understand social action to be structured justice, to see that people get a fair share of the blessings that God has given us."

T.V., properly maligned for feeding so much sawdust to the mind and the heart, will not let us forget the cruel starvation in Ethiopia and Sudan. It takes systems and structures and organizations to meet the needs of God's people, our sisters and brothers, on that massive scale. Whole church bodies, industry, and government need to band together to feed those who are now strangers in their own land, bedeviled by starvation, a cruelty intensified by governments fighting civil wars and hindering the food supplies from getting to the starving and the hungry. We have to see that this kind of starvation never happens again.

Individualism has been praised in our culture, and often in the church, and has, thereby, become an obstacle to needed community action. What is true about me is not so much that I am an *individual,* as that I am *related to you.* I am what I am, not because, "I believe in me," as one of the ads says. I am what I am because of what Christ has done for me. I am related to you because of what Christ has done to you. If that is true, I cannot stand by and watch you starve or be bent out of shape by injustice or watch your mind and heart lose vision because you don't have opportunities to learn.

What I am, is driven by this: "This interior resonance of recognition, begetting, or evoking praise and thanksgiving, is a function of the particularity of grace itself. For grace has its marks. Whenever men encounter grace it is the shock and the over-plus of sheer gratuity that announces the presence, as indeed, it invented the name. By gratuity is meant a primal surprise, the need-not-have-been of uncalculated and incalculable givenness. 'Amazing' is the only adequate adjective; wonder is the ambience. For amazement, wonder, and grace occur together. '. . . they were amazed at the graciousness of his words . . .' " (Joseph Sittler)

Amazed by the mighty hand and the outstretched arm, amazed by "Child of God, you are marked by the cross of Christ forever;" amazed by "My body, broken for you; my blood shed for you;" amazed by "As I have done this for you, so you also ought to do it for one another," we praise God and feed the neighbor.

To be identified, to know who we are and whose we are and what we are sent to do, that's Deuteronomic. That's contemporary. That's thanksgiving. Amen